CW00418987

by Iain Gray

Lang**Syne**
PUBLISHING
WRITING *to* REMEMBER

LangSyne

PUBLISHING

WRITING *to* REMEMBER

79 Main Street, Newtongrange,
Midlothian EH22 4NA
Tel: 0131 344 0414   Fax: 0845 075 6085
E-mail: info@lang-syne.co.uk
www.langsyneshop.co.uk

Design by Dorothy Meikle
Printed by Printwell Ltd
© Lang Syne Publishers Ltd 2018

ISBN 978-1-85217-242-8

Brennan

MOTTO:
By a strong hand.

CREST:
A mailed arm wielding a sword
(and) a plume of five ostrich feathers
rising out of a ducal coronet.

NAME variations include:
Ó Braonain *(Gaelic)*
MacBranan *(Gaelic)*
MacBranain *(Gaelic)*
O'Branain
O'Brennan
Brannan
Branny

Chapter one:
Origins of Irish surnames

**According to an old saying, there are two types of Irish –
those who actually are Irish and those who wish they were.**

This sentiment is only one example of the allure that the
high romance and drama of the proud nation's history holds
for thousands of people scattered across the world today.

It's a sad fact, however, that the vast majority of Irish
surnames are found far beyond Irish shores, rather than on
the Emerald Isle itself.

The population stood at around eight million souls in
1841, but today it stands at fewer than six million.

This is mainly a tragic consequence of the potato
famine, also known as the Great Hunger, which devastated
Ireland between 1845 and 1849.

The Irish peasantry had become almost wholly reliant
for basic sustenance on the potato, first introduced from the
Americas in the seventeenth century.

When the crop was hit by a blight, at least 800,000
people starved to death while an estimated two million
others were forced to seek a new life far from their native
shores – particularly in America, Canada, and Australia.

The effects of the potato blight continued until about
1851, by which time a firm pattern of emigration had
become established.

Ireland's loss, however, was to the gain of the countries in which the immigrants settled, contributing enormously, as their descendants do today, to the well being of the nations in which their forefathers settled.

But those who were forced through dire circumstance to establish a new life in foreign parts never forgot their roots, or the proud heritage and traditions of the land that gave them birth.

Nor do their descendants.

It is a heritage that is inextricably bound up in the colourful variety of Irish names themselves – and the origin and history of these names forms an integral part of the vibrant drama that is the nation's history, one of both glorious fortune and tragic misfortune.

This history is well documented, and one of the most important and fascinating of the earliest sources are *The Annals of the Four Masters*, compiled between 1632 and 1636 by four friars at the Franciscan Monastery in County Donegal.

Compiled from earlier sources, and purporting to go back to the Biblical Deluge, much of the material takes in the mythological origins and history of Ireland and the Irish.

This includes tales of successive waves of invaders and settlers such as the Fomorians, the Partholonians, the Nemedians, the Fir Bolgs, the Tuatha De Danann, and the Laigain.

Of particular interest are the *Milesian Genealogies*,

because the majority of Irish clans today claim a descent from either Heremon, Ir, or Heber – three of the sons of Milesius, a king of what is now modern day Spain.

These sons invaded Ireland in the second millennium B.C, apparently in fulfilment of a mysterious prophecy received by their father.

This Milesian lineage is said to have ruled Ireland for nearly 3,000 years, until the island came under the sway of England's King Henry II in 1171 following what is known as the Cambro-Norman invasion.

This is an important date not only in Irish history in general, but for the effect the invasion subsequently had for Irish surnames.

'Cambro' comes from the Welsh, and 'Cambro-Norman' describes those Welsh knights of Norman origin who invaded Ireland.

But they were invaders who stayed, inter-marrying with the native Irish population and founding their own proud dynasties that bore Cambro-Norman names such as Archer, Barbour, Brannagh, Fitzgerald, Fitzgibbon, Fleming, Joyce, Plunkett, and Walsh – to name only a few.

These 'Cambro-Norman' surnames that still flourish throughout the world today form one of the three main categories in which Irish names can be placed – those of Gaelic-Irish, Cambro-Norman, and Anglo-Irish.

Previous to the Cambro-Norman invasion of the twelfth century, and throughout the earlier invasions and settlement of those wild bands of sea rovers known as the Vikings in the eighth and ninth centuries, the population of the island was relatively small, and it was normal for a person to be identified through the use of only a forename.

But as population gradually increased and there were many more people with the same forename, surnames were adopted to distinguish one person, or one community, from another.

Individuals identified themselves with their own particular tribe, or 'tuath', and this tribe – that also became known as a clann, or clan – took its name from some distinguished ancestor who had founded the clan.

The Gaelic-Irish form of the name Kelly, for example, is Ó Ceallaigh, or O'Kelly, indicating descent from an original 'Ceallaigh', with the 'O' denoting 'grandson of.' The name was later anglicised to Kelly.

The prefix 'Mac' or 'Mc', meanwhile, as with the clans of the Scottish Highlands, denotes 'son of.'

Although the Irish clans had much in common with their Scottish counterparts, one important difference lies in what are known as 'septs', or branches, of the clan.

Septs of Scottish clans were groups who often bore an entirely different name from the clan name but were under the clan's protection.

In Ireland, septs were groups that shared the same name and who could be found scattered throughout the four provinces of Ulster, Leinster, Munster, and Connacht.

The 'golden age' of the Gaelic-Irish clans, infused as their veins were with the blood of Celts, pre-dates the Viking invasions of the eighth and ninth centuries and the Norman invasion of the twelfth century, and the sacred heart of the country was the Hill of Tara, near the River Boyne, in County Meath.

Known in Gaelic as 'Teamhar na Rí', or Hill of Kings, it was the royal seat of the 'Ard Rí Éireann', or High King of Ireland, to whom the petty kings, or chieftains, from the island's provinces were ultimately subordinate.

It was on the Hill of Tara, beside a stone pillar known as the Irish 'Lia Fáil', or Stone of Destiny, that the High Kings were inaugurated and, according to legend, this stone would emit a piercing screech that could be heard all over Ireland when touched by the hand of the rightful king.

The Hill of Tara is today one of the island's main tourist attractions.

Opposition to English rule over Ireland, established in the wake of the Cambro-Norman invasion, broke out frequently and the harsh solution adopted by the powerful forces of the Crown was to forcibly evict the native Irish from their lands.

These lands were then granted to Protestant colonists, or 'planters', from Britain.

Many of these colonists, ironically, came from Scotland and were the descendants of the original 'Scotti', or 'Scots', who gave their name to Scotland after migrating there in the fifth century A.D., from the north of Ireland.

Colonisation entailed harsh penal laws being imposed on the majority of the native Irish population, stripping them practically of all of their rights.

The Crown's main bastion in Ireland was Dublin and its environs, known as the Pale, and it was the dispossessed peasantry who lived outside this Pale, desperately striving to eke out a meagre living.

It was this that gave rise to the modern-day expression of someone or something being 'beyond the pale'.

Attempts were made to stamp out all aspects of the ancient Gaelic-Irish culture, to the extent that even to bear a Gaelic-Irish name was to invite discrimination.

This is why many Gaelic-Irish names were anglicised with, for example, and noted above, Ó Ceallaigh, or O'Kelly, being anglicised to Kelly.

Succeeding centuries have seen strong revivals of Gaelic-Irish consciousness, however, and this has led to many families reverting back to the original form of their name, while the language itself is frequently found on the fluent tongues of an estimated 90,000 to 145,000 of the island's population.

Ireland's turbulent history of religious and political strife is one that lasted well into the twentieth century, a landmark century that saw the partition of the island into the twenty-six counties of the independent Republic of

Ireland, or Eire, and the six counties of Northern Ireland, or Ulster.

Dublin, originally founded by Vikings, is now a vibrant and truly cosmopolitan city while the proud city of Belfast is one of the jewels in the crown of Ulster.

It was Saint Patrick who first brought the light of Christianity to Ireland in the fifth century A.D.

Interpretations of this Christian message have varied over the centuries, often leading to bitter sectarian conflict – but the many intricately sculpted Celtic Crosses found all over the island are symbolic of a unity that crosses the sectarian divide.

It is an image that fuses the 'old gods' of the Celts with Christianity.

All the signs from the early years of this new millennium indicate that sectarian strife may soon become a thing of the past – with the Irish and their many kinsfolk across the world, be they Protestant or Catholic, finding common purpose in the rich tapestry of their shared heritage.

Chapter two:
Sons of the little raven

**The proud name of Brennan in the form it has today
stems from the two quite distinct Gaelic forms of Ó
Braonain and Mac Branain.**

'Branain' indicates 'little raven', and it was in the area of
the east of the present day county of Roscommon that the
Mac Branains flourished for centuries.

Tracing a descent from Bragnan, a son of a Viking king
of Dublin, the Ó Braonain flourished in the area of present
day County Kilkenny, where they held sway as chiefs of the
territory of Idough.

These Vikings, known as Ostmen, had occupied and
fortified Dublin in the mid-ninth century and had other
important trading settlements on other parts of the island.

Other septs of both 'names' were also to be found
throughout the Emerald Isle, and what they all had in
common was not only a truly illustrious lineage but also a
fierce and stubborn determination to protect their ancient
rights and privileges.

It is through Eochu Muighmheadow, a mid-fourth century
A.D. Ard Rí, or High King of Ireland, that the Brennans of
today, through the Mac Branains, can trace a descent from the
legendary Irish hero gloriously and colourfully known as
Conn Céthchathach, or Conn of the Hundred Battles.

Ard Rí, or High King of Ireland from about 177 to 212 A.D. this ancestor of the Brennans of today figures prominently in what are known as the Fenian Cycle of tales, also known as the Ossianic Cycle and thought to date from the third century.

One of Conn's illustrious ancestors is said to have been no less than Goidel Glas, who is reputed to have created the Gaelic-Irish language after he combined and refined the 72 known languages of his time.

The result is the language of poets that thrills like the plucked strings of an Irish harp throughout the Fenian Cycle.

As a youth, Conn is said to have met two mysterious figures who predicted he and his descendants would rule Ireland.

The strange figures who are reputed by legend to have appeared to Conn, enshrouded in mist, were a beautiful young maiden known as Sovranty. Wearing a golden crown and seated on a crystal chair, she was accompanied by the sun god Lugh, patron of arts and crafts.

It is said they prophesied his descendants would rule until the death of the old Gods – which in fact did occur in the form of St. Patrick and the new religious pantheon of Christianity.

Conn attained the High Kingship after overthrowing Cathair Mór, also known as Mal, who had killed his father.

But his kingship was never secure because he had to

fight a relentless succession of battles with his great rival Eogan Mór, also known as Mug Nadhat, king of the Dál nAraide, or Cruithe, who occupied the northeastern territories of Ireland.

It was because of the number of battles Conn fought with these Cruithne, or Picts, that he earned the title of Conn Céthchathach – Conn of the Hundred Battles.

The two rival kings achieved a temporary accommodation after the island was divided between themselves, the division starting at a ridge known as Eiscir Riada, which traverses the island from Galway Bay to Dublin.

Mug's territory in the south was known as Leth Moga Nuadht, while Conn's northern territory was known as Leth Cuinn.

But it was not long before the ambitious and fiercely proud pair were at each other's throats again.

Mug gained the upper hand for a time after storing up grain in his territories after taking heed of a dire Druidic prophecy of famine – but Conn eventually defeated his rival after taking him by cunning surprise in a night raid near present-day Tullamore, in County Offaly.

Conn consolidated his kingship over Ireland, but his success was short-lived, destined to die under the glinting blades of fifty warriors who had managed to breach the defences of his royal bastion of Tara after disguising themselves as women.

At the head of these warriors was the vengeful Tibride

Tirech, son of the Cathair Mór whom Conn had killed years earlier in revenge for the death of his own father.

But Conn's great legacy would survive through the number of proud clans such as the Brennans that were spawned from his virile seed.

The 'Branain' from whom the Mac Branains ultimately took their name is thought to have lived from the mid to the latter years of the fourth century A.D. and it was his great grandson, the Archdruid Ona, who provides an enduring link with St. Patrick who, along with St. Bridget and St. Columcille, is one of Ireland's patron saints.

It was St. Patrick's fifth century mission to bring the light of Christianity to the island, ultimately eradicating worship of the old Celtic gods.

As a powerful member of the ancient Druid caste Ona, who ruled as chief in an area of present day Co. Roscommon that was known as Corca Achlann, would have understandably been opposed to the saint's evangelising mission.

Undaunted by Ona's hostile reception of him, St. Patrick decided that Corca Achlann would be an ideal site for the establishment of one of his churches.

The wily Ona asked him what he could expect in payment for granting him land, to which the saint replied: 'A portion of heavenly country for that earthly country.'

Distinctly unimpressed, Ona informed him that he was only interested in solid gold as payment.

The saint then wandered over to a spot where a pig had recently been rooting in the ground and there, to the astonishment of those present, lay a lump of gold.

St. Patrick offered it to Ona as payment – but with the warning that he would never be a king, or any of his descendants.

Alarmed by this, a rather contrite Ona then granted the saint the site of one of his forts on which to build his church – with no payment required.

According to one ancient account of the incident the saint is then said to have 'blessed Ona and his posterity, on account of his penance and liberality, promising, and in promising having the power of an oracle, foretelling for certain that from Ona's seed many men distinguished in the arts of war and the sacred pursuits of peace would be descended.'

The strange prophecy was fulfilled over succeeding centuries as the Mac Branains, although never kings in their own right, ruled as chieftains in Corca Achlann as trusted kinsfolk of the powerful O'Connor kings of the province of Connacht.

This bond with the O'Connors was to prove very much a double-edged sword as the Brennans shared in both the glorious fortunes and the tragic misfortunes of the O'Connor kings.

A stunning blow to the ancient Gaelic way of life of proud clans such as the Brennans and the O'Connors came with the late twelfth century Norman invasion of Ireland.

This was an invasion that led to English dominion over the island being ratified through the Treaty of Windsor of 1175, under the terms of which the O'Connor king Rory O'Connor, for example, was allowed to rule territory unoccupied by the Normans – but only in the role of a vassal of the English king.

Chapter three:
Rivalry and rebellion

As the English grip on Ireland tightened, the island groaned under a weight of oppression that was directed in the main against native Irish clans such as the Brennans.

An indication of the harsh treatment meted out to them can be found in a desperate plea sent to Pope John XII by Roderick O'Carroll of Ely, Donald O'Neil of Ulster, and a number of other Irish chieftains in 1318.

They stated: 'As it very constantly happens, whenever an Englishman, by perfidy or craft, kills an Irishman, however noble, or however innocent, be he clergy or layman, there is no penalty or correction enforced against the person who may be guilty of such wicked murder.

'But rather the more eminent the person killed and the higher rank which he holds among his own people, so much more is the murderer honoured and rewarded by the English, and not merely by the people at large, but also by the religious and bishops of the English race.'

Adding to the misery of the Brennans of Corca Achlann, was that they became embroiled in not only vicious disputes among branches of the O' Connors, but among themselves.

Rivalry over who should be the Brennan chieftain led to

a bloody encounter in 1411 at a spot later known as Beal Atha na mBuille, meaning 'the mouth of the ford of the strokes', with 'strokes' indicating the sword strokes of battle.

This gave rise to the name of the present day town of Strokestown.

As the Brennans battled among themselves, the power of the English Crown only increased, leading to frequent outbreaks of bloody rebellion.

These were uprisings against English rule in which all the different septs of Brennans scattered throughout Ireland played a role.

This was to have truly devastating consequences not only for the Brennans but other native Irish clans.

Discontent had grown over the policy known as 'plantation', or settlement of loyal Protestants on lands previously held by the native Irish.

This policy had started during the reign from 1491 to 1547 of Henry VIII, whose Reformation effectively outlawed the established Roman Catholic faith throughout his dominions.

This plantation continued throughout the subsequent reigns of Elizabeth I, James I (James VI of Scotland), Charles I, and in the aftermath of the Cromwellian invasion of the island in 1649.

Rebellion erupted in 1594 against the increasingly harsh treatment of the native Irish at its forefront was the

O'Donnell chieftain Aodh Rua Ó Domhmaill, better known
to posterity as Red Hugh O'Donnell.

In what became known as the Cogadh na Naoi
mBliama, or the Nine Years War, Red Hugh and his allies
literally set the island ablaze in a vicious campaign of
guerrilla warfare.

In 1596, allied with the forces of Hugh O'Neill, Earl of
Tyrone, Red Hugh and his Gallagher cavalry inflicted a
defeat on an English army at the battle of Clontibert, while
in August of 1598 another significant defeat was inflicted at
the battle of Yellow Ford.

As English control over Ireland teetered on the brink of
collapse, thousands of more troops, including mercenaries,
were hastily despatched to the island and, in the face of the
overwhelming odds against them, Red Hugh and the Earl of
Tyrone sought help from England's enemy, Spain.

A well-equipped Spanish army under General del
Aquila landed at Kinsale in December of 1601, but was
forced into surrender only a few weeks later, in January of
1602.

Resistance continued until 1603, but proved abortive.

Four years later, in September of 1607 and in what is
known as The Flight of the Earls, main leaders of the
rebellion sailed into foreign exile from the village of
Rathmullan, on the shore of Lough Swilly, in Co. Donegal,
accompanied by ninety loyal followers.

In an insurrection that exploded in 1641, at least 2,000

Protestant settlers were massacred at the hands of Catholic landowners and their native Irish peasantry, while thousands more were stripped of their belongings and driven from their lands to seek refuge where they could.

Terrible as the atrocities were against the Protestant settlers, subsequent accounts became greatly exaggerated, serving to fuel a burning desire on the part of Protestants for revenge against the rebels.

Tragically for Ireland, this revenge became directed not only against the rebels, but the native Irish such as the Brennans in general.

The English Civil War intervened to prevent immediate action against the rebels, but following the execution of Charles I in 1649 and the consolidation of the power of England's fanatically Protestant Oliver Cromwell, the time was ripe for revenge.

The Lord Protector, as he was named, descended on Ireland at the head of a 20,000-strong army that landed at Ringford, near Dublin, in August of 1649.

The consequences of this Cromwellian conquest still resonate throughout the island today.

Cromwell had three main aims: to quash all forms of rebellion, to 'remove' all Catholic landowners who had taken part in the rebellion, and to convert the native Irish to the Protestant faith.

An early warning of the terrors that were in store for the native Catholic Irish came when the northeastern town of

Drogheda was stormed and taken in September and between 2,000 and 4,000 of its inhabitants killed, including priests who were summarily put to the sword.

The defenders of Drogheda's St. Peter's Church, who had also refused to surrender, were burned to death as they huddled for refuge in the steeple and the church was deliberately torched.

A similar fate awaited Wexford, on the southeast coast, where at least 1500 of its inhabitants were slaughtered, including 200 defenceless women, despite their pathetic and heart-rending pleas for mercy.

Three hundred other inhabitants of the town drowned when their overladen boats sank as they desperately tried to flee to safety, while a group of Franciscan friars were massacred in their church – some as they knelt before the altar.

Cromwell soon held Ireland in a grip of iron, allowing him to implement what amounted to a policy of ethnic cleansing.

His troopers were given free rein to hunt down and kill priests, while estates such as those of many Brennans were confiscated and 'planted' by loyal Protestants.

Further rebellions would follow, and in there grim aftermath many Brennans who had not been able to arrive at a suitable accommodation with the powerful forces of the English Crown were destined to seek a new life on foreign shores.

Chapter four:

On the world stage

Far removed from the grim hardships and bitter strife of earlier centuries, many Brennans flourished, and continue to flourish, in a diverse range of pursuits.

Born in 1932 in Los Angeles, **Eileen Brennan** is the American stage, film, television actress and singer whose first major stage role was in the 1959 *Little Miss Sunshine*.

This was followed with the role of Irene Malloy in the original Broadway production in 1964 of *Hello, Dolly!*

Her first appearance on the silver screen was in *Divorce American Style* while she also made appearances on the American television variety show *Rowan and Martin's Laugh-In*.

Other movie roles include *The Sting*, from 1973, *The Last Picture Show*, the 1978 *The Cheap Detective* and the 1980 *Private Benjamin*, for which she received an Oscar nomination.

The film was later adapted for a television series, for which she received an Emmy award.

The multi-talented actress has also appeared in the American television series *7th Heaven* and *Will and Grace*.

The winner of no less than three Academy Awards, **Walter Brennan** was the American actor born in 1894 in Swampscott, Massachusetts, and who died in 1974.

Of Irish stock, Brennan followed in his father's footsteps by studying engineering.

But with his eye on the stage, the young Brennan also performed occasionally in Vaudeville before enlisting in the ranks of the American Army during the First World War.

It was while serving on active duty in France that his vocal chords were damaged and he aged prematurely because of the terrible effects of mustard gas.

Returning from the war he became involved in a number of ultimately unsuccessful business ventures.

He eked out a living by taking bit parts in movies and also working as a stuntman – but by 1936 he had won his first Academy Award for Best Supporting Actor for his role as Swan Bostrom in *Come and Get It*.

Another Academy Award followed in 1938 for his role in *Kentucky* and, two years later, for his role in *The Westerner* – making him the only actor to date to have won three Academy Awards for Best Supporting Actor.

A veteran of 230 film and television roles, most notably in Westerns, he has a star on the Hollywood Walk of Fame.

In the world of the printed word **Maeve Brennan**, born in 1917 in Dublin, was the Irish-American writer who became renowned for her beauty, style, wit, and intelligence.

Her father, **Robert Brennan**, born in 1881 and who died in 1964, was a prominent Irish Republican who was imprisoned for a time for his part in the abortive Easter Rising of 1916, followed by further terms of imprisonment.

The family moved to Washington in 1934 when Robert Brennan was appointed the Irish Free State's first minister to the United States, and Maeve remained in the country after her family later returned to Ireland.

She began to write for the celebrated magazine *The New Yorker* under the pseudonym of 'The Long-Winded Lady', with her first short story, *The Holy Terror*, published in 1950.

Tragedy struck in the 1970s when, suffering from alcoholism and mental illness, she became destitute, wandering the streets of New York and staying in a number of transient hotels.

She died in 1993.

Born in 1918 **Joseph Payne Brennan** was a master of the genres of horror and fantasy and also an acclaimed poet.

His first published poem was the 1940 *When Snow Is Hung*, while he began writing horror and fantasy fiction for the *Weird Tales* magazine in 1952.

He was the author of classic spine-chilling tales such as *Slime* and *Canavan's Back Yard* and that other master of the horror genre, Stephen King, has written of how Brennan was a major influence on his own career and style as a writer. He died in 1990.

From horror and fantasy to the occult and mysticism James Herbert Brennan, better known as **J.H. Brennan** or 'Herbie Brennan' is the internationally acclaimed 'New Age' author whose was born in Ireland in 1940.

He is the author of more than 100 non-fiction and fiction books, including the 1971 *Astral Doorways*, the 1974 *Occult Reich*, and the 1982 *A Guide to Megalithic Ireland*.

Born in Sydney in 1870 **Christopher Brennan** was the Australian poet who is best remembered for his *Poems: 1913*, while **T. Casey Brennan**, born in 1948, is the American comic book writer who during the 1980s campaigned for depictions of smoking in magazines to be banned.

This led to then Arkansas Governor and future American President Bill Clinton issuing a proclamation declaring 'T. Casey Brennan Month' throughout the state.

In the world of ecclesiastical affairs **Denis Brennan**, born in Enniscorthy, Co. Wexford, in 1945 and who was ordained as a priest in 1970, is, at the time of writing, Bishop of Ferns.

Daniel Brennan, born in 1942, is the British life peer and barrister who, at the time of writing, is president of the Catholic Union of Great Britain.

Brennans have also excelled in the world of invention, and no less so than **Louis Brennan**, born in 1852 in Castlebar, Ireland, and who later immigrated to Australia.

He was the inventor of the **Brennan Torpedo**, the world's first guided missile. Patented by the inventor in 1877, it was taken up by the British government to protect the nation's coastal defences.

His fertile brain also produced a gyroscopically

balanced monorail system for military use, in addition to pioneering work on what would later become the helicopter.

Created a Companion of the Order of the Bath in 1892, his genius was extinguished forty years later after he was killed in a road accident.

On the field of battle **Joseph Brennan**, born in 1836, was an English recipient of the Victoria Cross, the highest award for gallantry for British and Commonwealth forces.

He had been a bombardier with the Royal Regiment of Artillery when in April of 1858, during the Indian Mutiny, he directed accurate and devastating fire on the enemy during their assault on the defences of Jhansi.

Later promoted to the rank of sergeant, he died in 1872.

From the field of battle to the often equally vicious field of politics another **Joseph Brennan**, born in 1912 in Donegal and who died in 1980, was the Irish Fianna Fáil party politician who held a number of important Irish Republic positions that included Minister for Posts and Telegraphs, Minister for Social Welfare, and Minister for Labour.

Born in 1928 in Rockhampton, Queensland, **Sir Gerald Brennan** is the eminent lawyer and judge who served as 10th Chief Justice of Australia from between 1995 to 1998.

In the highly competitive world of sport **Colt Brennan**, born in 1982 in Laguna Beach, California, is the talented American football quarterback who, at the time of writing, plays for the University of Hawaii.

Brian Brennan, born in 1952 in Bloomfield, Michigan,

is the former American football wide receiver who played for teams that included the Cleveland Browns, the Cincinnati Bengals, and the San Diego Chargers.

From American football to European football **Killian Brennan**, born in 1984 in Drogheda, is the Irish left-winger nicknamed 'Killer' who, at the time of writing, plays for League of Ireland club Derry City.

Across the ocean to Canada **Jim Brennan**, born in East York, Ontario in 1977 is one of the few Canadian football players to have played in the English Premier League.

He played for clubs that included Bristol City, Nottingham Forest, and Southampton, before returning to Canada in 2007 to play for Toronto Football Club.

On the cricket field **Donald Brennan**, born in 1920 in Eccleshill, Yorkshire, and who died in 1985, was the English batsman who played in two Test Matches in 1951, while in the world of ice hockey **Kip Brennan**, born in 1980 in Kingston, Ontario, is the talented hockey player who, at the time of writing, plays for Washington Capitals AHL affiliate.

Born in 1975 in Toowoomba, Queensland, **Michael Brennan** is the Australian field hockey player nicknamed 'Mouse.'

He was a member of the Australian men's team that took a bronze medal at the 1971 Olympics in Sydney, while four years later the midfielder was a member of the team that took the gold medal at the 2004 Olympics in Athens.

Born in 1900 in Brooklyn, New York, **Joseph Brennan** was one of the first professional American basketball players, while **Frank Brennan**, born in 1960 in Liverpool, is a world-class master of karate.

In the rough and tumble of the sport of hurling **Eddie Brennan**, born in 1978, is the Irish hurler who is the recipient of a number of awards while **Nickey Brennan**, born in 1953, is the former hurling player and manager who, at the time of writing, is president of the Irish Gaelic Athletic Association.

To end on a musical note, **Clannad** is the internationally renowned Irish group from Gweedore, in Co. Donegal.

Winners of a prestigious Grammy Award in 1997 for Best New Age Album for their album *Landmarks*, the band are composed of siblings Máire Brennan, Ciarán Brennan, and Pól Brennan and musicians Noel and Pádraig Duggan.

One of the Brennan sisters, **Enya**, born in 1964, is the multi-talented composer, instrumentalist, singer, and producer, who is also one of the biggest selling female artistes in recording history.

Key dates in Ireland's history from the first settlers to the formation of the Irish Republic:

circa 7000 B.C.	Arrival and settlement of Stone Age people.
circa 3000 B.C.	Arrival of settlers of New Stone Age period.
circa 600 B.C.	First arrival of the Celts.
200 A.D.	Establishment of Hill of Tara, Co. Meath, as seat of the High Kings.
circa 432 A.D.	Christian mission of St. Patrick.
800-920 A.D.	Invasion and subsequent settlement of Vikings.
1002 A.D.	Brian Boru recognised as High King.
1014	Brian Boru killed at battle of Clontarf.
1169-1170	Cambro-Norman invasion of the island.
1171	Henry II claims Ireland for the English Crown.
1366	Statutes of Kilkenny ban marriage between native Irish and English.
1529-1536	England's Henry VIII embarks on religious Reformation.
1536	Earl of Kildare rebels against the Crown.
1541	Henry VIII declared King of Ireland.
1558	Accession to English throne of Elizabeth I.
1565	Battle of Affane.
1569-1573	First Desmond Rebellion.
1579-1583	Second Desmond Rebellion.
1594-1603	Nine Years War.
1606	Plantation' of Scottish and English settlers.

1607	Flight of the Earls.
1632-1636	Annals of the Four Masters compiled.
1641	Rebellion over policy of plantation and other grievances.
1649	Beginning of Cromwellian conquest.
1688	Flight into exile in France of Catholic Stuart monarch James II as Protestant Prince William of Orange invited to take throne of England along with his wife, Mary.
1689	William and Mary enthroned as joint monarchs; siege of Derry.
1690	Jacobite forces of James defeated by William at battle of the Boyne (July) and Dublin taken.
1691	Athlone taken by William; Jacobite defeats follow at Aughrim, Galway, and Limerick; conflict ends with Treaty of Limerick (October) and Irish officers allowed to leave for France.
1695	Penal laws introduced to restrict rights of Catholics; banishment of Catholic clergy.
1704	Laws introduced constricting rights of Catholics in landholding and public office.
1728	Franchise removed from Catholics.
1791	Foundation of United Irishmen republican movement.
1796	French invasion force lands in Bantry Bay.
1798	Defeat of Rising in Wexford and death of United Irishmen leaders Wolfe Tone and Lord Edward Fitzgerald.

1800	Act of Union between England and Ireland.
1803	Dublin Rising under Robert Emmet.
1829	Catholics allowed to sit in Parliament.
1845-1849	The Great Hunger: thousands starve to death as potato crop fails and thousands more emigrate.
1856	Phoenix Society founded.
1858	Irish Republican Brotherhood established.
1873	Foundation of Home Rule League.
1893	Foundation of Gaelic League.
1904	Foundation of Irish Reform Association.
1913	Dublin strikes and lockout.
1916	Easter Rising in Dublin and proclamation of an Irish Republic.
1917	Irish Parliament formed after Sinn Fein election victory.
1919-1921	War between Irish Republican Army and British Army.
1922	Irish Free State founded, while six northern counties remain part of United Kingdom as Northern Ireland, or Ulster; civil war up until 1923 between rival republican groups.
1949	Foundation of Irish Republic after all remaining constitutional links with Britain are severed.